The Open-String Book for Bass

by Cassia Harvey

CHP355

©2019 by C. Harvey Publications All Rights Reserved.
www.charveypublications.com
www.learnstrings.com

The Open-String Book for Bass

1. Open G String

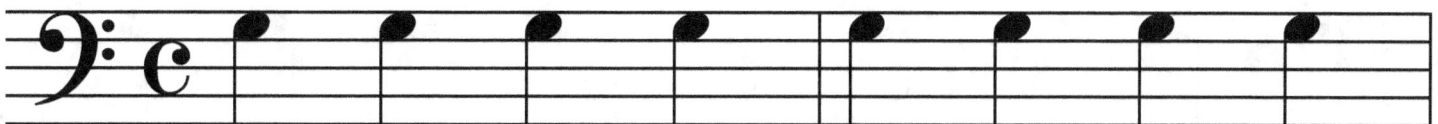

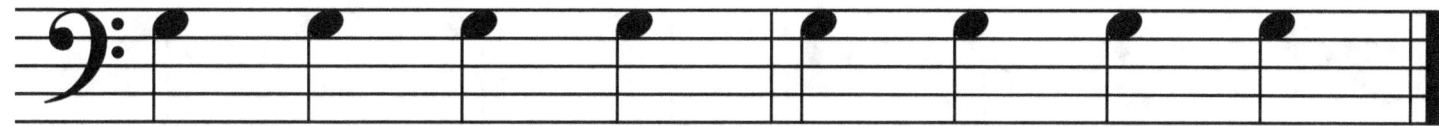

2. Open G with Rests

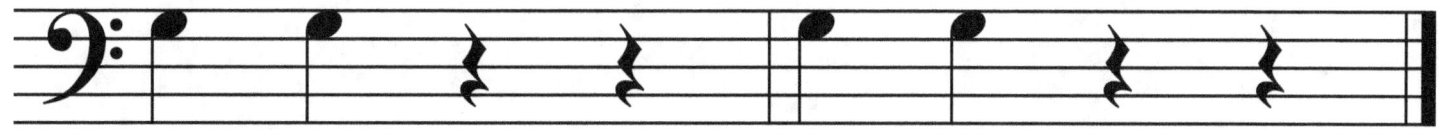

©2019 C. Harvey Publications All Rights Reserved.

3. Open G with More Rests

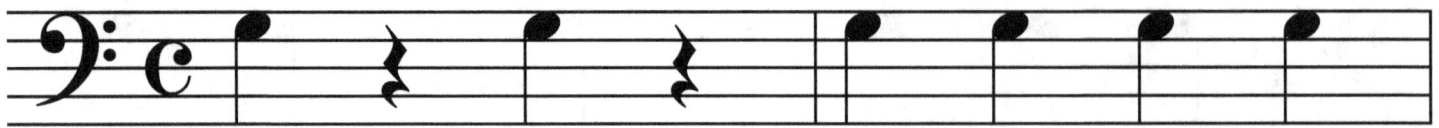
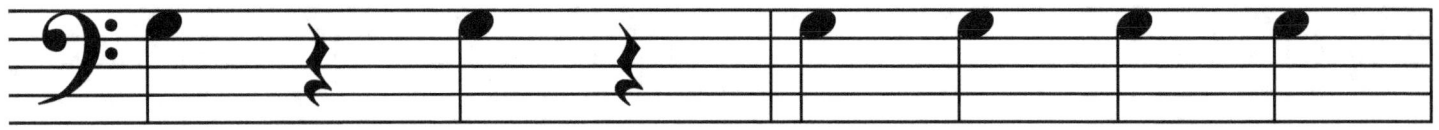
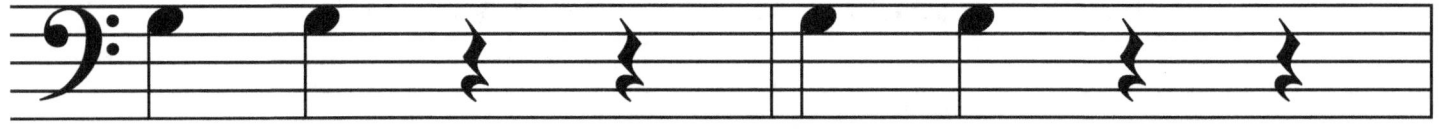
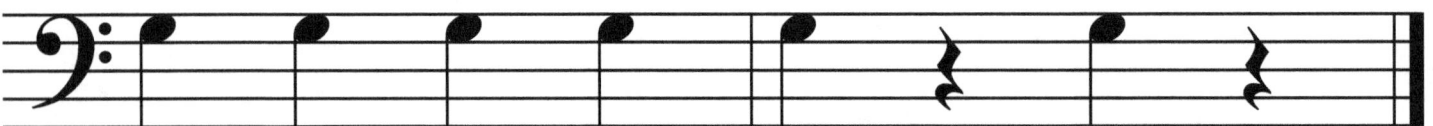

4. Open D String

5. Open D with Long-Short-Short

6. Open D with Rests

7. Open D with Half Notes

8. Open G and D

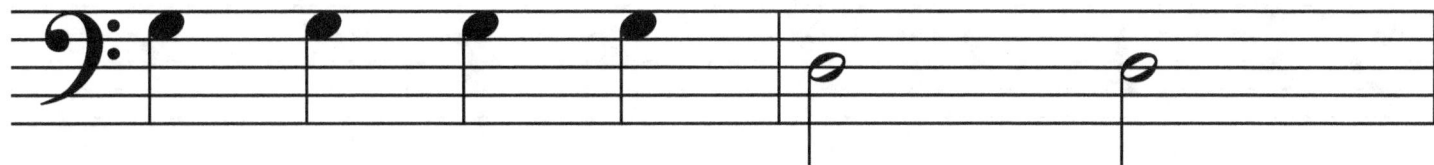

9. Open G and D Double Stops

10. Open A String

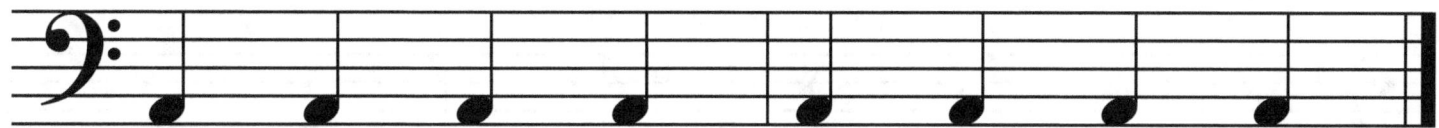

11. Open A with Short-Short-Long

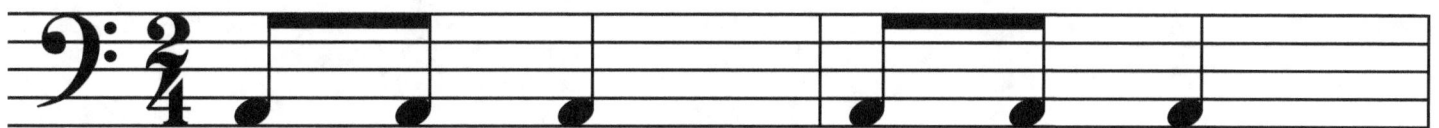

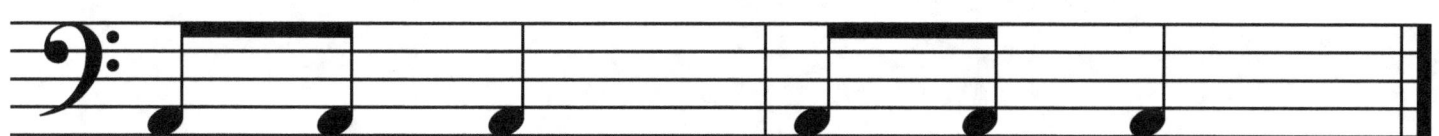

12. Open A with Rests

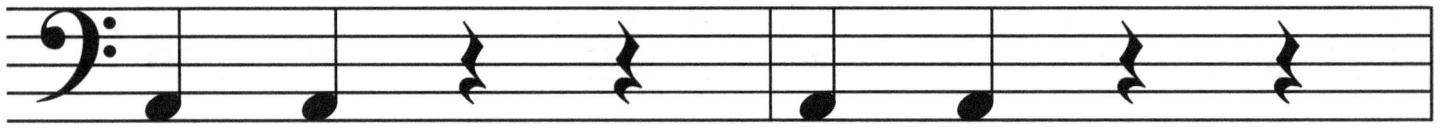
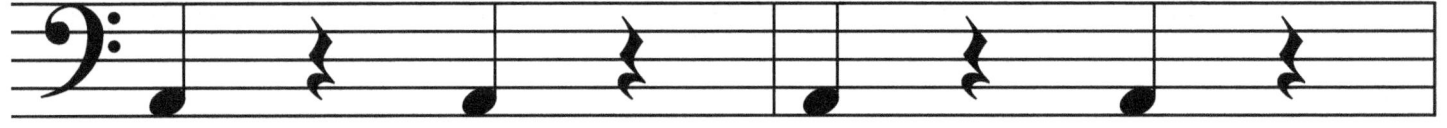
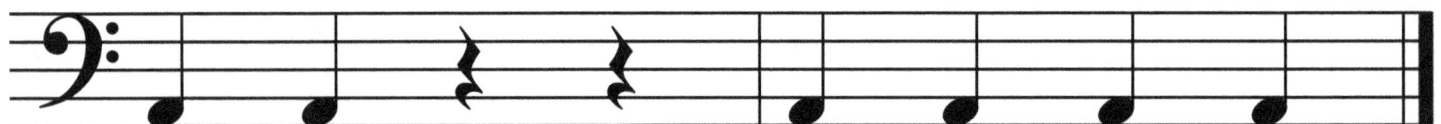

13. Open A and D

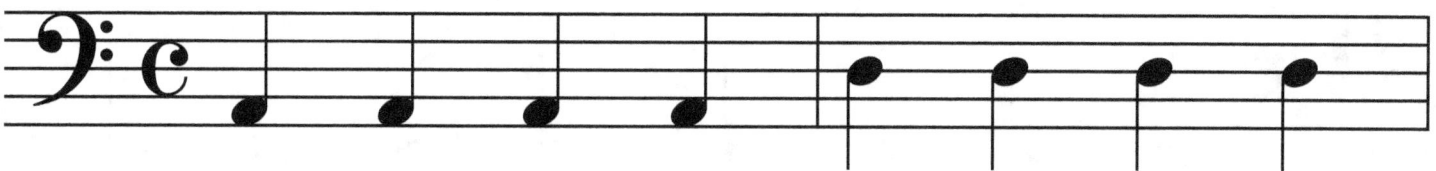
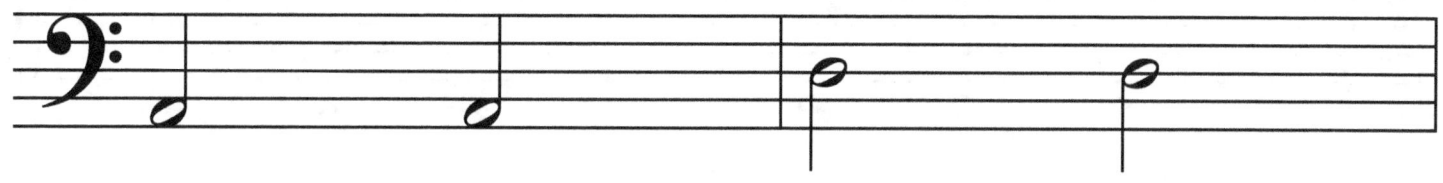

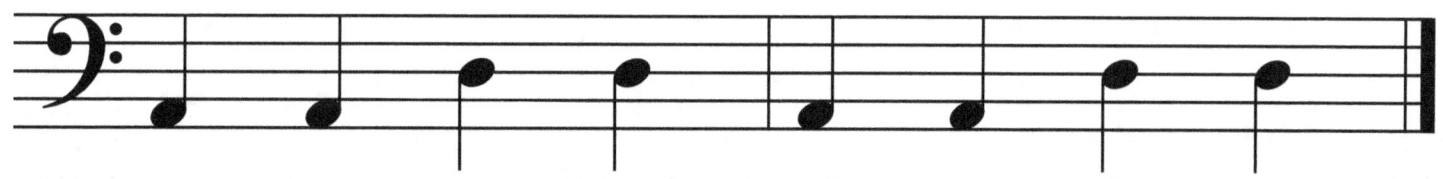

14. Open E

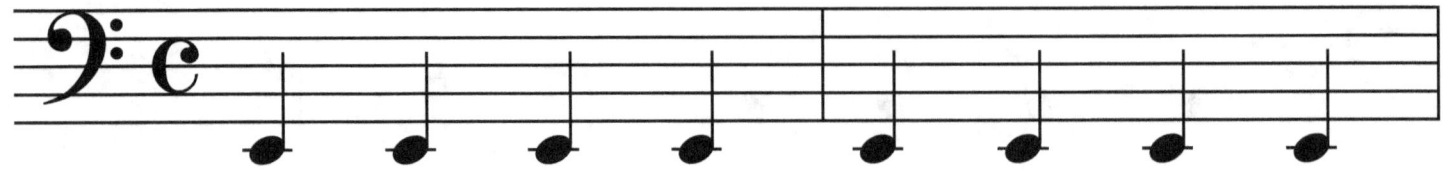

15. Open E with Rests

16. Open E with Short-Short-Long

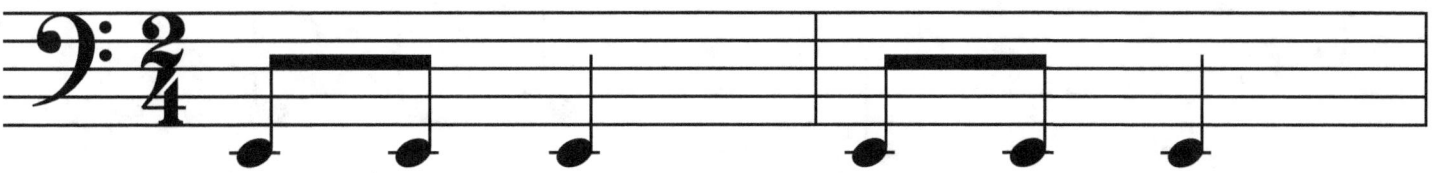
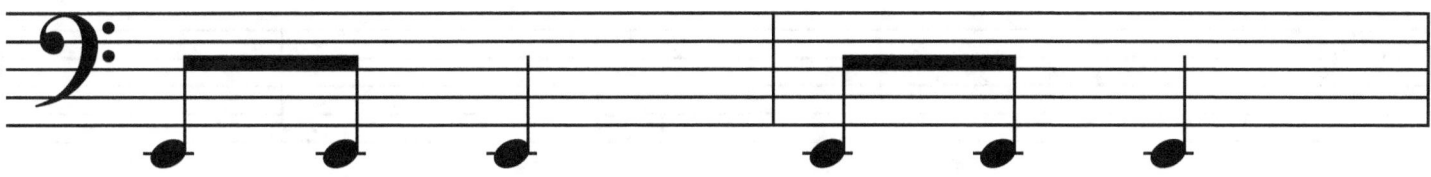
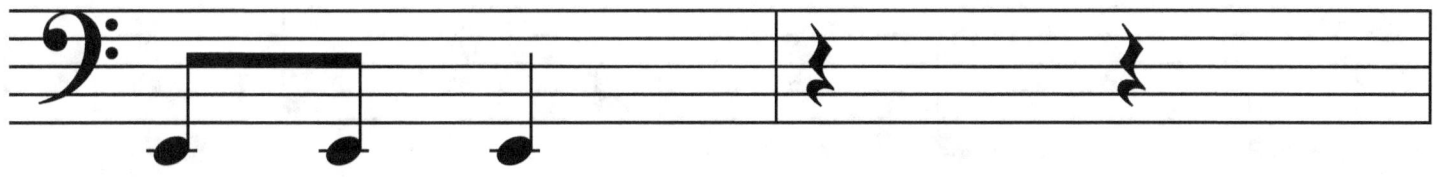

17. Open E and A

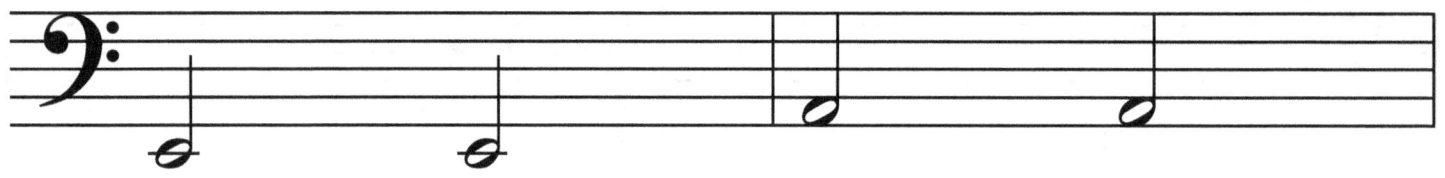

18. Double Stops on G and D

19. Double Stops on D and A

20. Double Stops on A and E

21. Marching in Double Stops

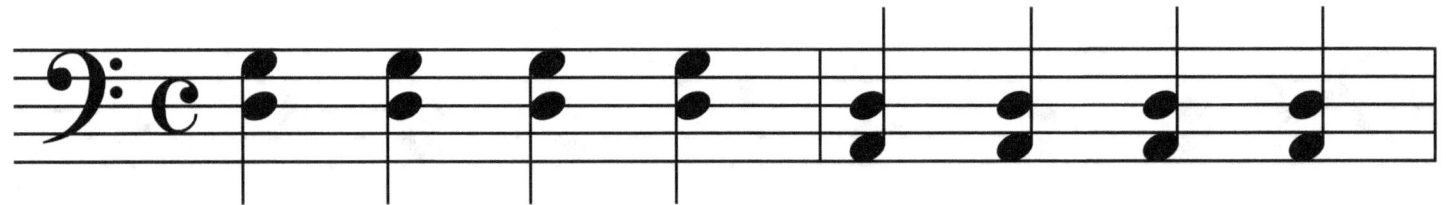
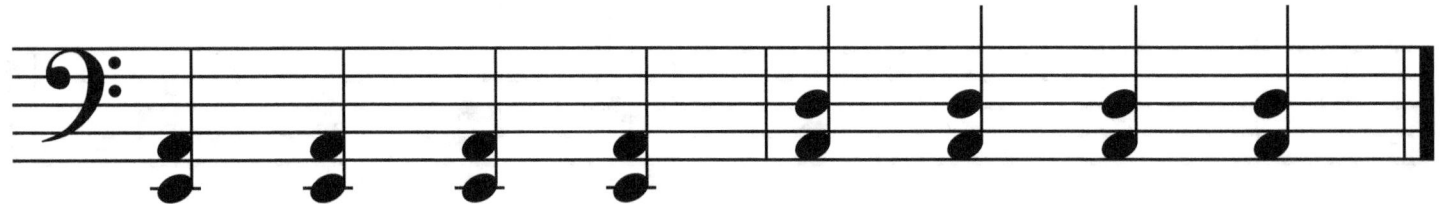

22. Counting to 3

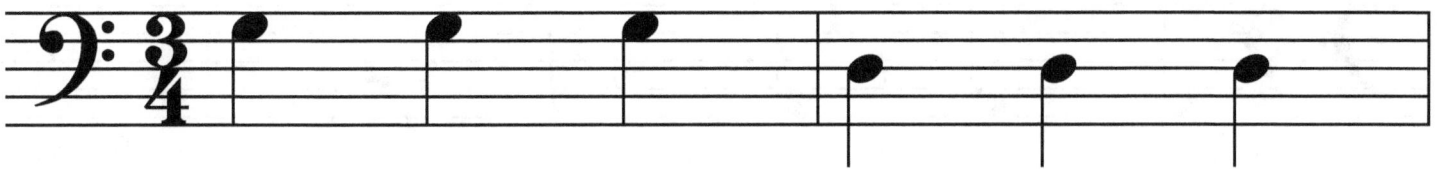

23. Three Beats in a Measure

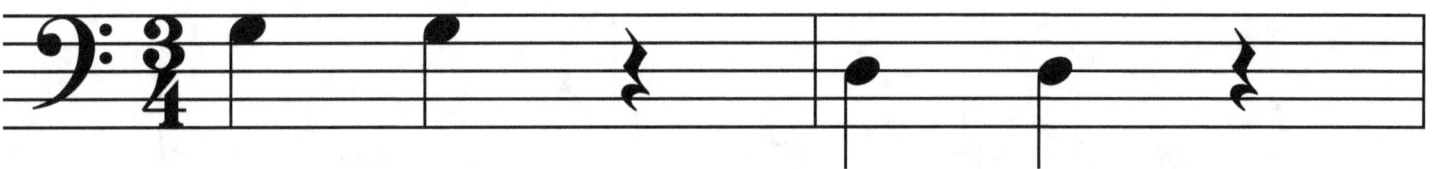

24. Three Beats on E

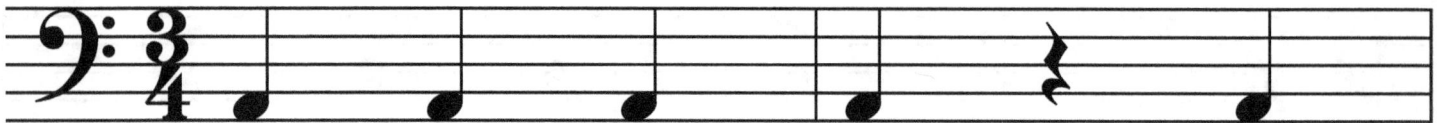

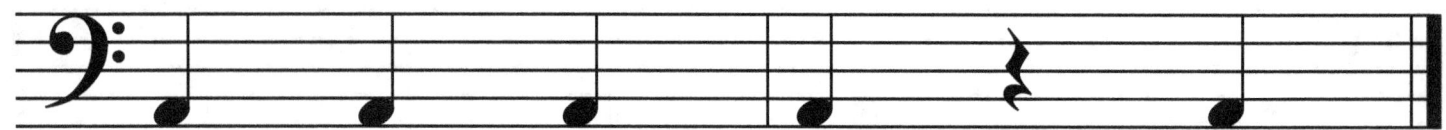

25. Three Beats on E

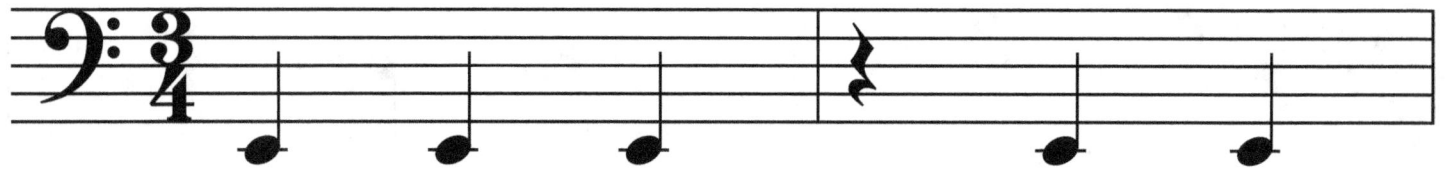

26. Three Beats in a Measure

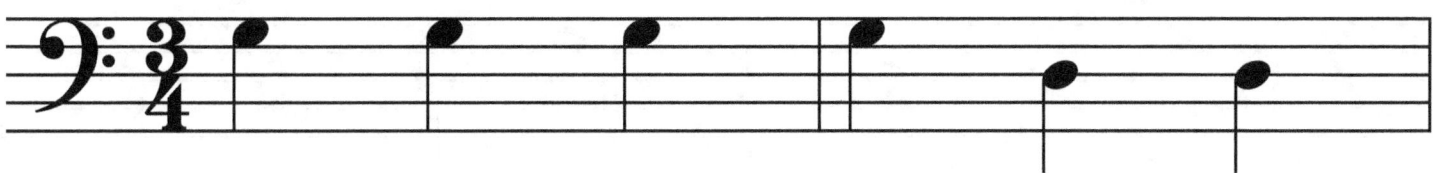

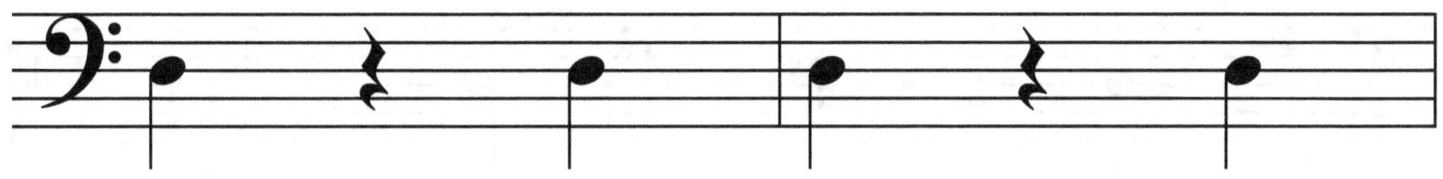

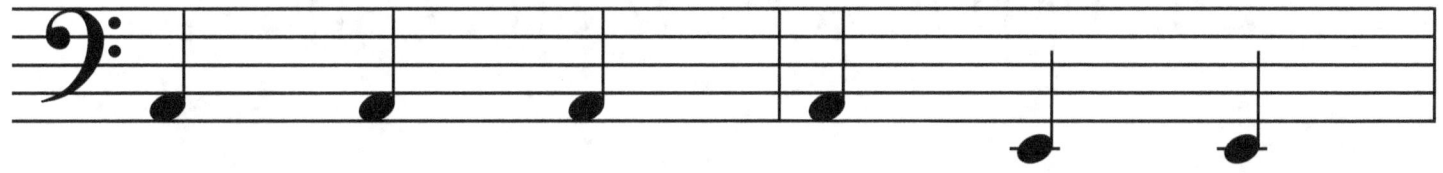

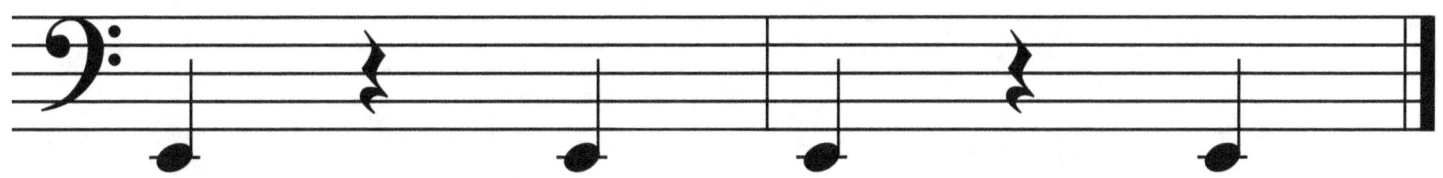

27. Two in a Bow on G and D

28. Two in a Bow on D and A

29. Two in a Bow on A and E

30. Two in a Bow on D and G

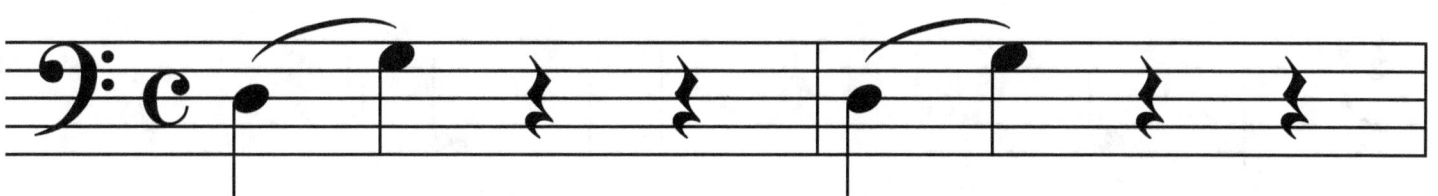

31. Two in a Bow on A and D

32. Two in a Bow on E and A

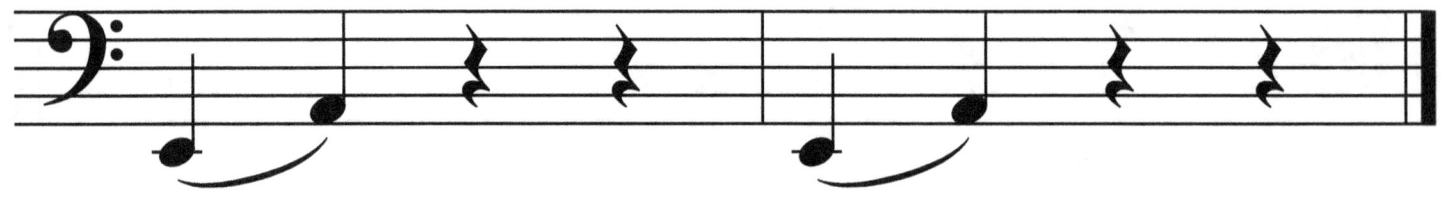

33. Two in a Bow without Rests

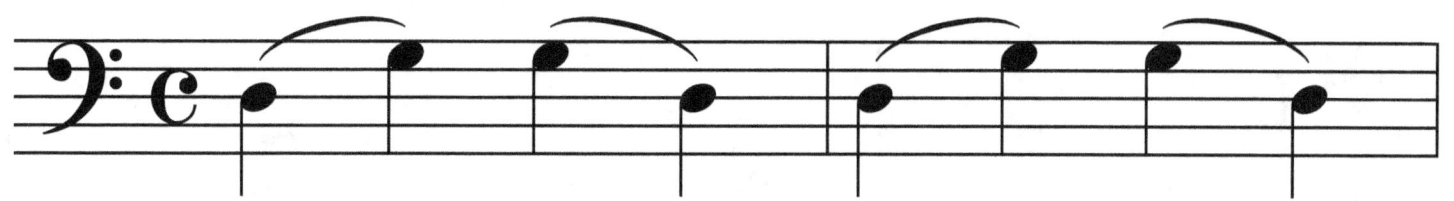

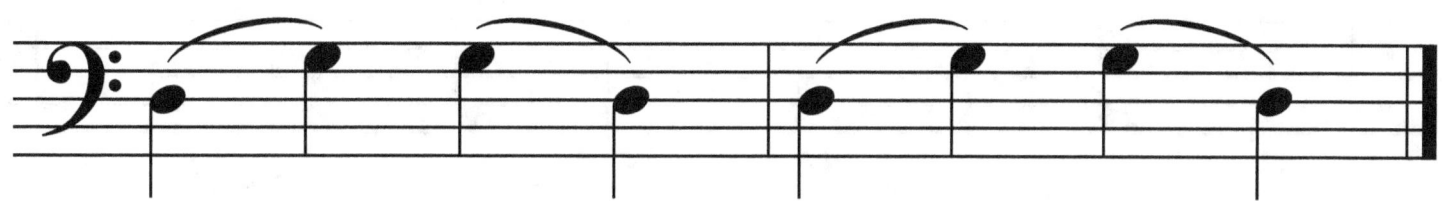

34. Two in a Bow on A and D

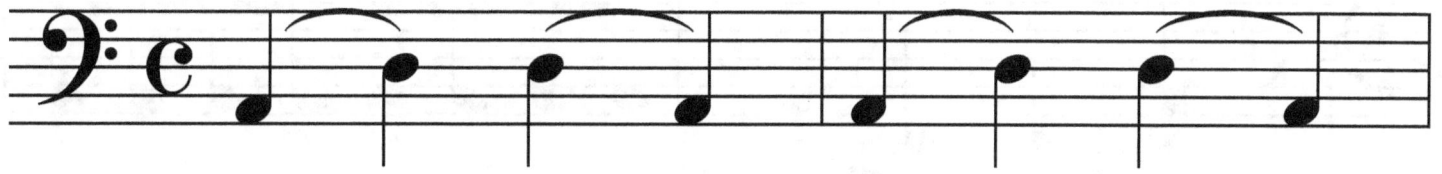

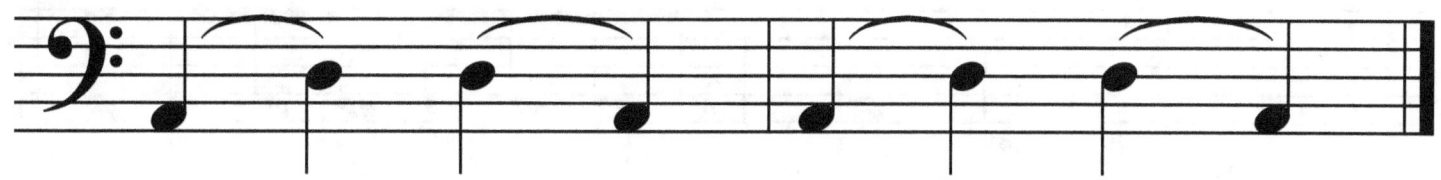

35. Two in a Bow on E and A

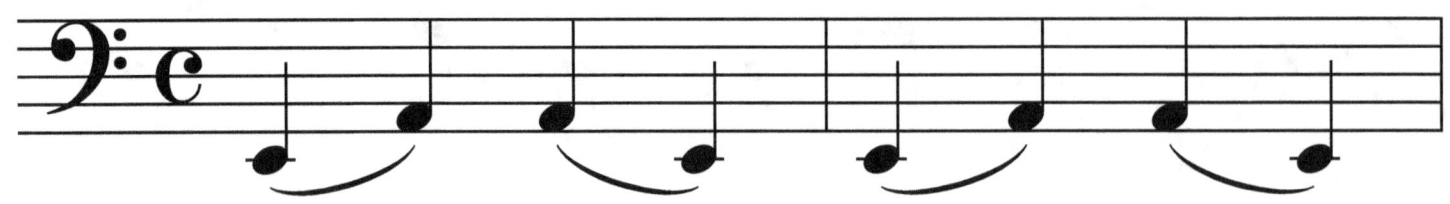

36. Slow and Fast Bows on A and E

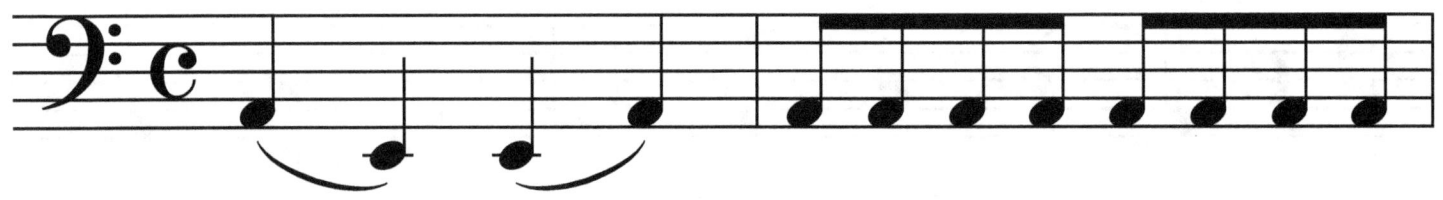

37. Slow and Fast Bows on D and A

38. Slow and Fast Bows on A and G

39. Two in a Bow Exercise

40. Whole Notes

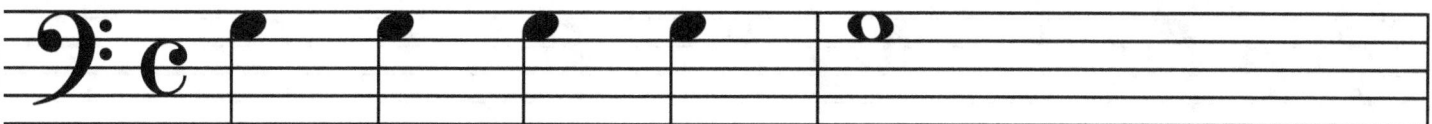

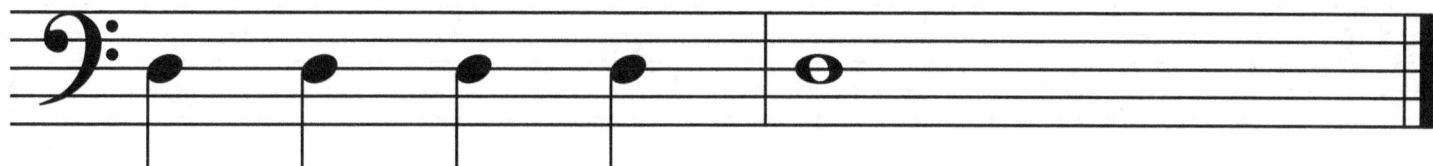

41. Half Notes and Whole Notes

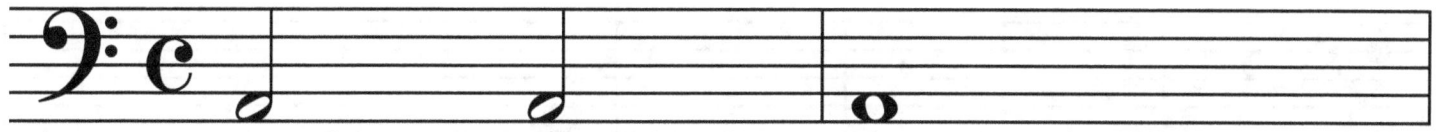

42. Counting to 1, 2, and 4

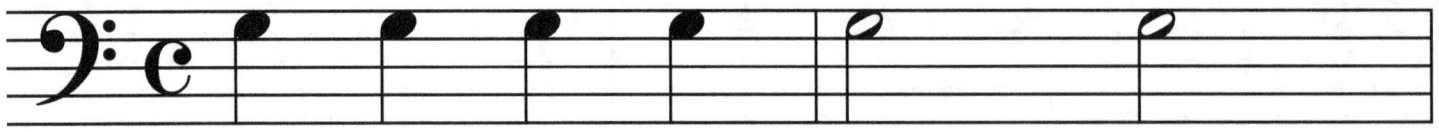
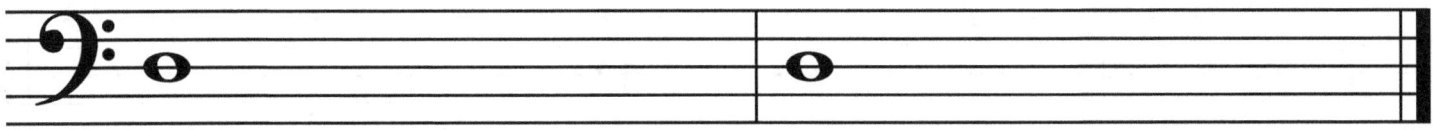

43. Counting to 1, 2, and 4

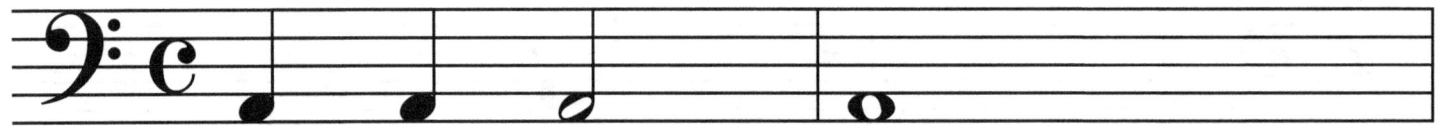

44. Counting to 1, 2, and 4

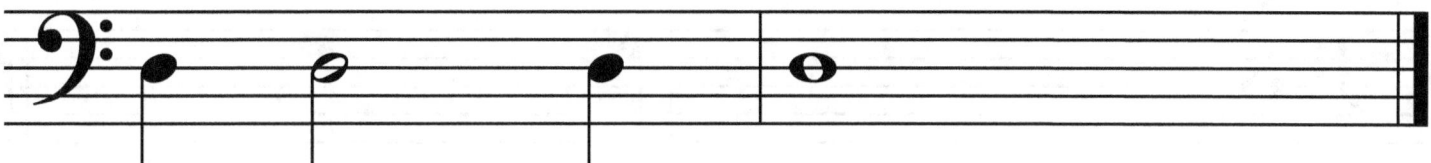

45. Counting to 1, 2, and 4

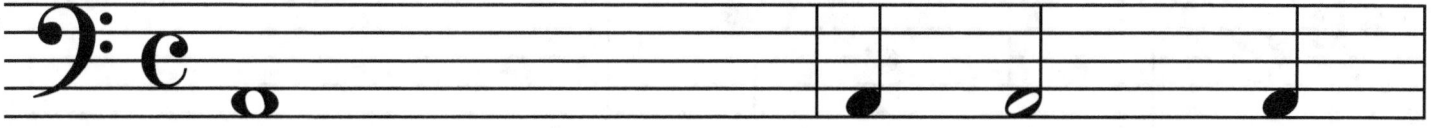

46. Counting and String Crossing

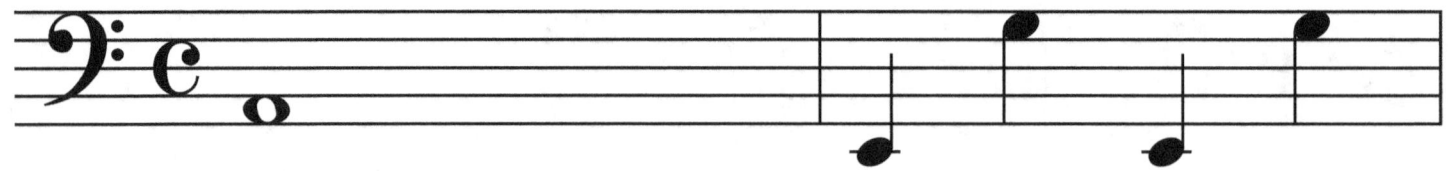

47. More Counting and String Crossing

48. Putting it all Together on G and D

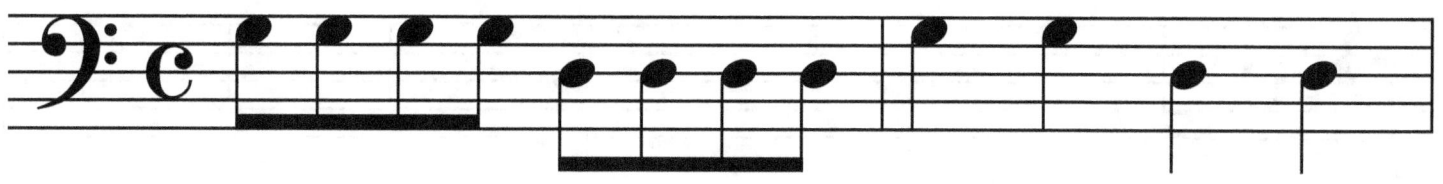

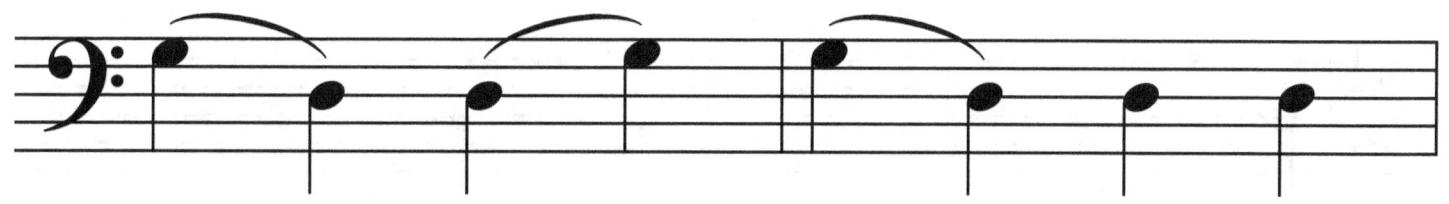

49. Putting it all Together on D and A

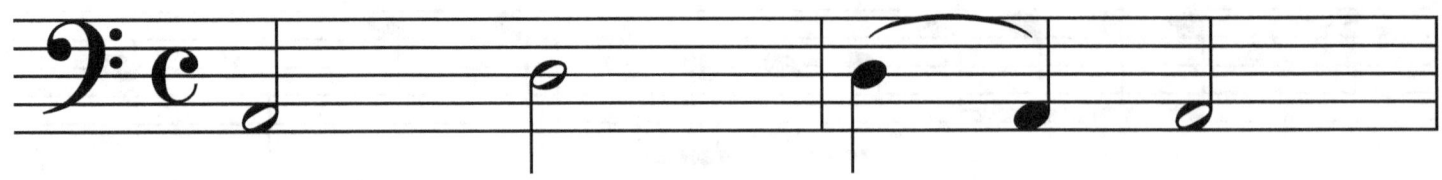

50. Putting it all Together on A and E

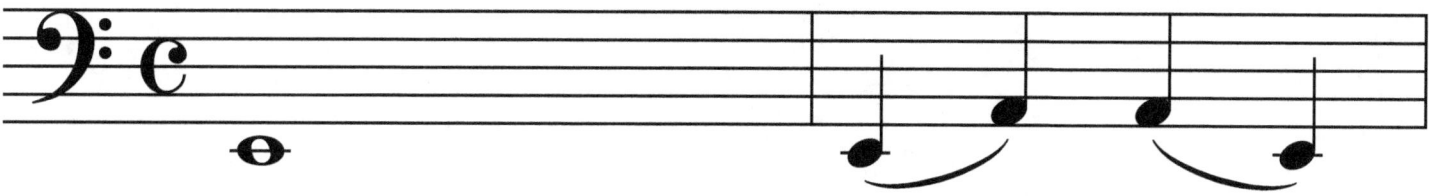
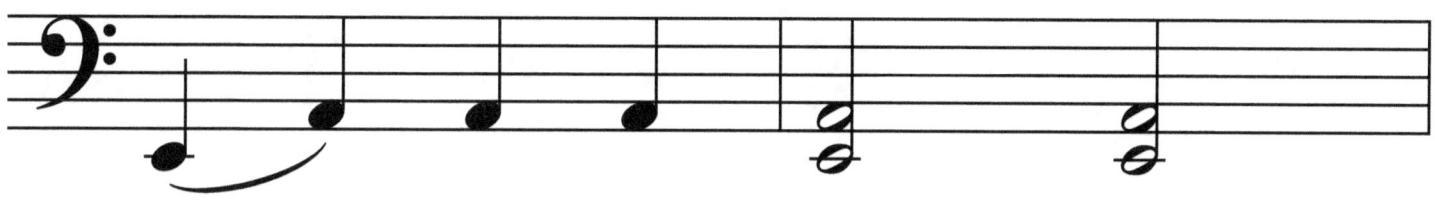
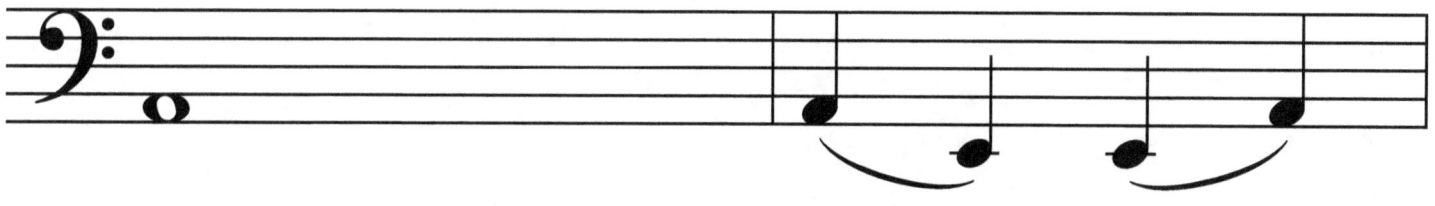